Quick! Draw a policeman to catch him!

What made him slip?

How will he get across?

Who or what is she waiting for?

What have these tourists come to see?

It's a shipwreck!

Draw a forest! Is there a wolf?

What do you want the robot to do?

Whose legs are these?

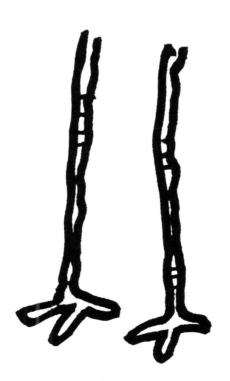

Surprise! (Draw the surprise.)

What is he throwing?

Who's in this balloon?

Draw two more goats, a bridge, and a troll.

What are they arguing about?

Something is on the other side of a wall. What is it?

The little robot wants to tell you something.

What's she scared of?

Something has fallen from the airplane!

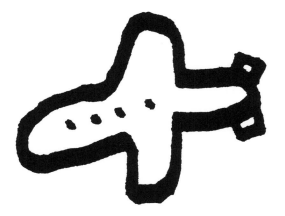

What's going on?

Let's take a helicopter ride!

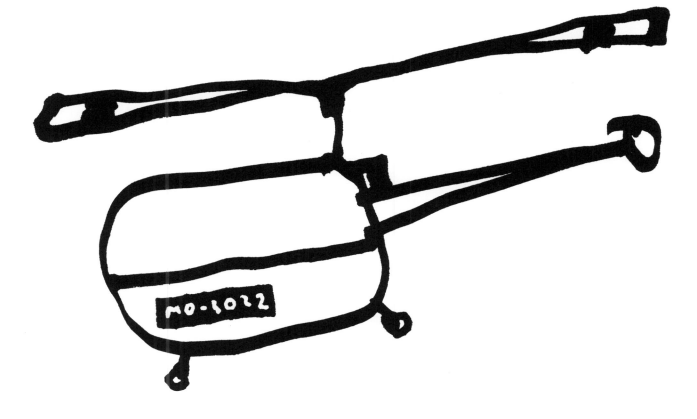

What is the baby thinking?

She has a lot to say. What's she talking about?

What have you got in those tweezers?

This is the beginning of his story:

What's so funny?

I want to tell you something!

What's the best news you heard this year?

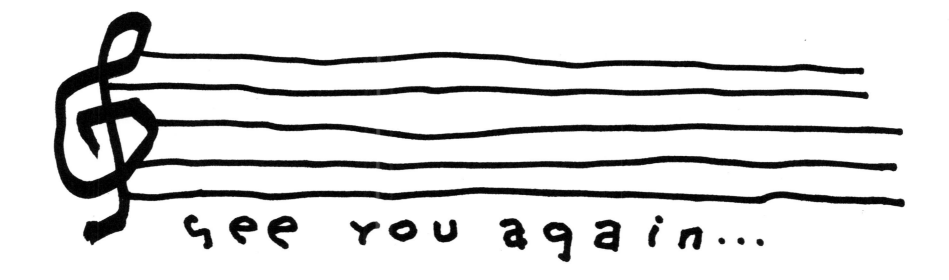

Give these books titles.

What time did you go to bed last night? What did you dream about?

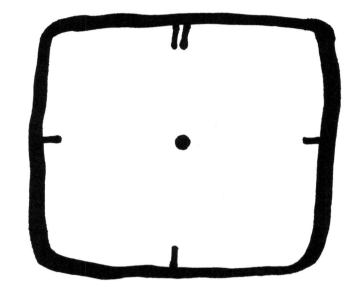

Who lives here?

Something is falling down the stairs.

What did he trip on?

Poor Cinderella! Be her fairy godmother and cast a spell on her.

What's that on the sand dune?!

When you write the book of your life, what will the cover look like?

What did he bump into?

Scare the dog away!

When I was your age . . .

What is she daydreaming about?

Let's listen to what Mr. Pig has to say.

What's floating down the river?

This hand is holding a tool. What's the tool for?